SEALS, SEA LIONS
& WALRUSES

Published by Creative Education, Inc., 123 South Broad Street, Mankato, Minnesota 56001

Printed by permission of Wildlife Education, Ltd.

ISBN 0-88682-271-8

SEALS, SEA LIONS & WALRUSES

Created and Written by
John Bonnett Wexo

Zoological Consultant
Charles R. Schroeder, D.V.M.
Director Emeritus
San Diego Zoo &
San Diego Wild Animal Park

Scientific Consultants
Hubbs-Sea World Research Institute
San Diego, California

Creative Education

Art Credits

Pages Eight and Nine: Walter Stuart; Pages Ten and Eleven: Walter Stuart; Page Ten: Bottom Left, and Page Eleven: Top, Middle Right and Bottom Right, Graham Allen; Pages Twelve and Thirteen: Walter Stuart; Page Twelve: Middle Left and Bottom Left, and Page Thirteen: Top Right and Bottom, Graham Allen; Pages Sixteen and Seventeen: Walter Stuart; Page Sixteen: Middle Left, and Page Seventeen: Top and Bottom Right, Graham Allen; Pages Twenty and Twenty-one: Walter Stuart; Page Twenty: Bottom Left and Page Twenty-one: Top Right and Bottom Right, Graham Allen.

Photographic Credits

Cover: Francois Gohier *(Ardea London)*; Pages Six and Seven: G. L. Kooyman *(Animals Animals)*; Page Ten: Top, Cristopher Crowley *(Tom Stack & Assoc.)*; Middle, Kevin Schafer *(Tom Stack & Assoc.)*; Page Eleven: Top, C. Allan Morgan *(Peter Arnold, Inc.)*; Middle, Robert Evans *(Peter Arnold, Inc.)*; Page Thirteen: Middle Right, Bob Evans *(Peter Arnold, Inc.)*; Middle Left, Kevin Schafer *(Tom Stack & Assoc.)*; Pages Fourteen and Fifteen: Dotte Larsen *(Bruce Coleman Inc.)*; Page Sixteen: Top, Jen & Des Bartlett *(Bruce Coleman Inc.)*; Middle Left, Jen & Des Bartlett *(Bruce Coleman Inc.)*; Bottom Left, S. J. Krasemann (DRK *Photo)*; Page Seventeen: E. R. Degginger *(Animals Animals)*; Pages Eighteen and Nineteen: Michael Fogden *(Animals Animals)*; Page Twenty: Top, Leonard Lee Rue III *(Animals Animals)*; Middle, Tom Stack *(Tom Stack & Assoc.)*; Page Twenty-one: Top Right, Mark Newman *(Tom Stack & Assoc.)*; Middle, Med Beauregard (PPS); Bottom Left, S. J. Krasemann (DRK *Photo)*; Page Twenty-two and Twenty-three: Ron and Valerie Taylor *(Ardea London)*.

Our Thanks To: Dr. Brian E. Joseph *(Sea World)*; Phyllis Evans; Don Kroll *(Scripps Institute)*; Dr. Lanny Cornell *(Sea World)*; and Lynnette Wexo.

Creative Education would like to thank Wildlife Education, Ltd., for granting them the rights to print and distribute this hardbound edition.

Contents

Seals, sea lions & walruses live in two different "worlds." They spend part of their lives on land, and part of their lives in water. On land, they may look clumsy. But in the water, they can swim with a speed and grace that is truly wonderful to watch. In fact, many species swim so well that they seem to "fly under water."

To help them swim, these animals have flippers instead of arms and legs. The flippers look like fins, and this is why seals, sea lions and walruses are all called *pinnipeds* (PIN-UH-PEDZ). The word means "fin-footed."

In general, pinnipeds have cigar-shaped bodies that slip through the water easily. The bodies are filled with strong muscles, and this helps to make the animals very good swimmers. Some pinnipeds can swim long distances, and some can dive deep to find food.

Pinnipeds are marine mammals. Like people and other land mammals, pinnipeds have lungs and must breathe air to stay alive. Like you and me, they are warm-blooded, with a body temperature that must be kept at a certain level all the time. Their babies are born alive like human babies. And the babies get milk from their mothers. Like many land mammals, pinnipeds have hair covering their bodies.

Most pinnipeds live in cold places. For instance, many seals and walruses are found close to the North Pole. And there are seals in waters near the South Pole. In such places, seals often spend long periods of time swimming under huge blocks of ice looking for food (like the seal shown at right).

In fact, most people think of snow and ice when they think of seals and other pinnipeds. But there are seals and sea lions that live in warm places as well. There are sea lions in California, for instance. And there are seals in Hawaii and the Mediterranean Sea.

Adult male pinnipeds are called "bulls." Adult females are called "cows." Baby seals are called "pups" until they are about five months old—and then they are called "yearlings." A young walrus is called a "calf."

There is more variety among pinnipeds than you might expect. All of their bodies are the same general shape—but the patterns of fur on the bodies and the shapes of their heads can be very different. There is also a great variety of sizes. The biggest of all is the Elephant seal. Males of this species can be almost 20 feet long (6 meters). And they can weigh up to 8 *thousand pounds* (3700 kilograms).

SOUTHERN SEA LION
Otaria byronia

WALRUS
Odobenus rosmarus

NORTHERN FUR SEAL
Callorhinus ursinus

HARP SEAL AND PUP
Phoca groenlandica

RINGED SEAL
Phoca hispida

BEARDED SEAL
Erignathus barbatus

CRABEATER SEAL
Lobodon carcinophagus

WEDDELL SEAL
Leptonychotes weddelli

8

HOODED SEAL
Cystophora cristata

SOUTHERN ELEPHANT SEAL
Mirounga leonina

NORTHERN ELEPHANT SEAL
Mirounga angustirostris

LEOPARD SEAL
Hydrurga leptonyx

STELLER'S SEA LION
Eumetopias jubatus

CALIFORNIA SEA LION
Zalophus californianus

RIBBON SEAL
Phoca fasciata

MEDITERRANEAN MONK SEAL
Monachus monachus

9

The bodies of all pinnipeds do look very much the same at first glance. All of them have long and rather streamlined bodies, shaped like fat submarines. And they all have four flippers—one pair in front and one pair in the back. Almost all pinnipeds are covered with fur. And they have long hairs on their faces that look like the whiskers on cats.

With so many things that are similar, you may think that it's going to be very hard for you to tell one kind of pinniped from another. But don't let it worry you. There are some differences between them that are going to make it *easy* for you to tell one from another. In fact, you'll be able to tell the difference in only a few seconds.

The easiest pinniped to recognize is the walrus. For one thing, it is bigger than any other pinniped, except the Elephant seal. And walruses are the only pinnipeds that have long tusks. Later on in this book, we're going to tell you about some other things that make walruses different.

But right now, we want to show you some ways that you can quickly tell a seal from a sea lion or a fur seal.

THIS IS A _____

THIS IS A _____

When you see a pinniped, look at its head. Does it have ears or not? Sea lions and fur seals have tiny earlobes, but true seals do not. For this reason, sea lions and fur seals are sometimes called "eared seals." Can you tell which of the animals shown at left is a true seal—and which one is a sea lion?

TRUE SEAL

SEA LION

SEA LION

TRUE SEAL

When sea lions and fur seals swim, they use their *front* flippers to push them through the water. Their rear flippers are used like the rudder on a boat, to help steer them.

True seals use their *rear* flippers to push them when they swim. The front flippers are used for steering.

SEA LION

True seals can't use their rear flippers like legs. And this can make them rather clumsy when they move around on land. Some species use their front flippers to pull them along. Others hunch their bodies and move like inch worms. But in spite of this, some types of seals may travel many miles on land. And some of them can move very fast. Crabeater seals can outrun a man in a race.

Sea lions and fur seals can use *both* pairs of their flippers to walk on land. They bring the rear flippers forward, so they look like long feet. For this reason, they can move fairly well on land—but they aren't nearly as graceful as they can be in the water.

TRUE SEAL

All pinnipeds can open and close their noses. When they stick their heads out of the water or come up on land, they can open their nostrils to breathe Ⓐ. But when they dive, they close the nostrils to keep water out Ⓑ.

Ⓑ

Ⓐ

Since you live on land, the natural position for your nostrils is open. But pinnipeds spend a great deal of time under water, so the natural position for their nostrils is *closed*. They have special muscles that can open the nostrils when they want to breathe. But the moment they relax these muscles, the nostrils snap shut.

One reason why many pinnipeds look like chubby cigars is that they have a thick layer of fat under the skin. This fat helps to keep them warm when they swim in cold water or lie on snow and ice.

BLUBBER

The fat under the skin is called *blubber*. Walruses have more blubber than any other pinnipeds, and this is one reason why they are bigger. The fat on a large walrus can be 6 inches thick in places (15 centimeters). And it can weigh *over 900 pounds* (410 kilograms) all by itself!

WALRUS

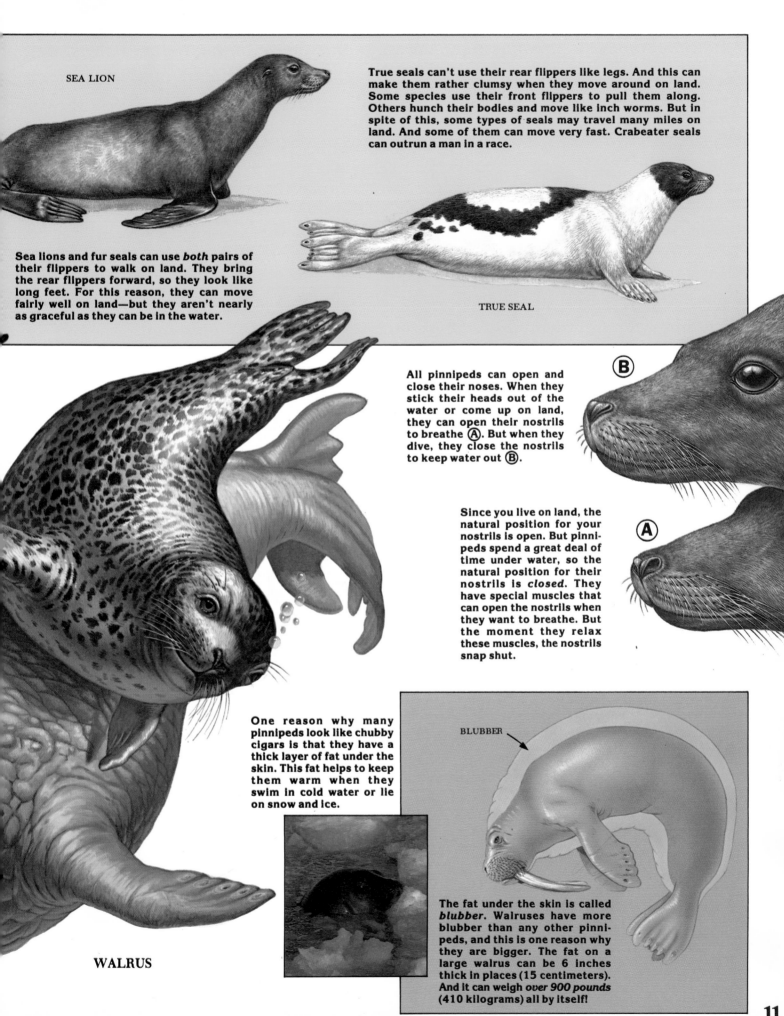

True seals are the largest group of pinnipeds, with more different kinds than any other group. As you can see on the map at right, they also live in more places than any other pinnipeds.

No matter where they live, true seals stay alive by eating fish and other sea creatures. Like all pinnipeds, they are excellent hunters. They usually have no trouble catching all the smaller animals they can eat. In turn, seals and other pinnipeds are sometimes caught by animals that are larger than they are—such as Killer whales.

PACIFIC OCEAN

ATLANTIC OCEAN

Places where seals live are shown in yellow.

As a rule, male seals are larger than females. Can you find the male Elephant seal in this picture?

At mating time, the males of some species fight with each other. The males that win the most fights get the most females as mates.

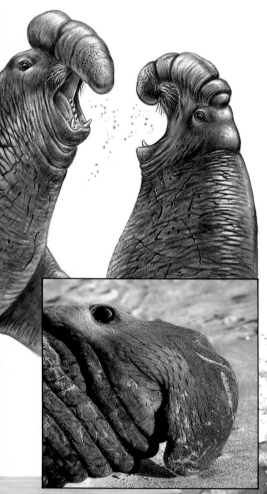

It's easy to see how the Elephant seal got its name. The "trunks" on some large males can be more than 11 inches long (28 centimeters). Sometimes, when the males get really angry, they may blow up their "trunks" like big balloons.

Killer whales have a clever way of capturing seals that are resting on ice floes. One whale pushes up the side of the ice (as shown at left). The seals tumble off —and land in the open mouth of a second whale.

In general, seals and other pinnipeds live in certain places because they can find plenty of food there. Pinnipeds are near the top of the "food chain" in the ocean. This chain begins with very small animals and plants Ⓐ.

Near the top of the chain, fish that have been eating smaller animals are eaten in turn by pinnipeds Ⓒ.

Ⓒ

The smallest animals and plants are eaten by slightly larger animals Ⓑ. And these are eaten by still larger animals.

Favorite foods of seals are squid and medium-sized fish.

PACIFIC OCEAN

INDIAN OCEAN

Life in the ocean can be very dangerous for seals and other pinnipeds. In cold waters, Killer whales hunt them. In warmer waters, they also have to worry about sharks.

To find food, a seal in cold waters may have to swim around under the ice for a long time. Some seals can hold their breath for *almost an hour*. But finally, they have to find a hole in the ice so they can get some air.

Seals and most other pinnipeds have very large eyes. This is probably because they need good eyesight to catch their prey.

Seals that use breathing holes usually have several of them. When ice forms over the holes, the seals dig it out with their teeth and claws. Or they may melt it with their warm breath. Polar bears and eskimos often hunt seals by waiting at breathing holes, as shown at right. When the seals come to breathe, the hunters catch them.

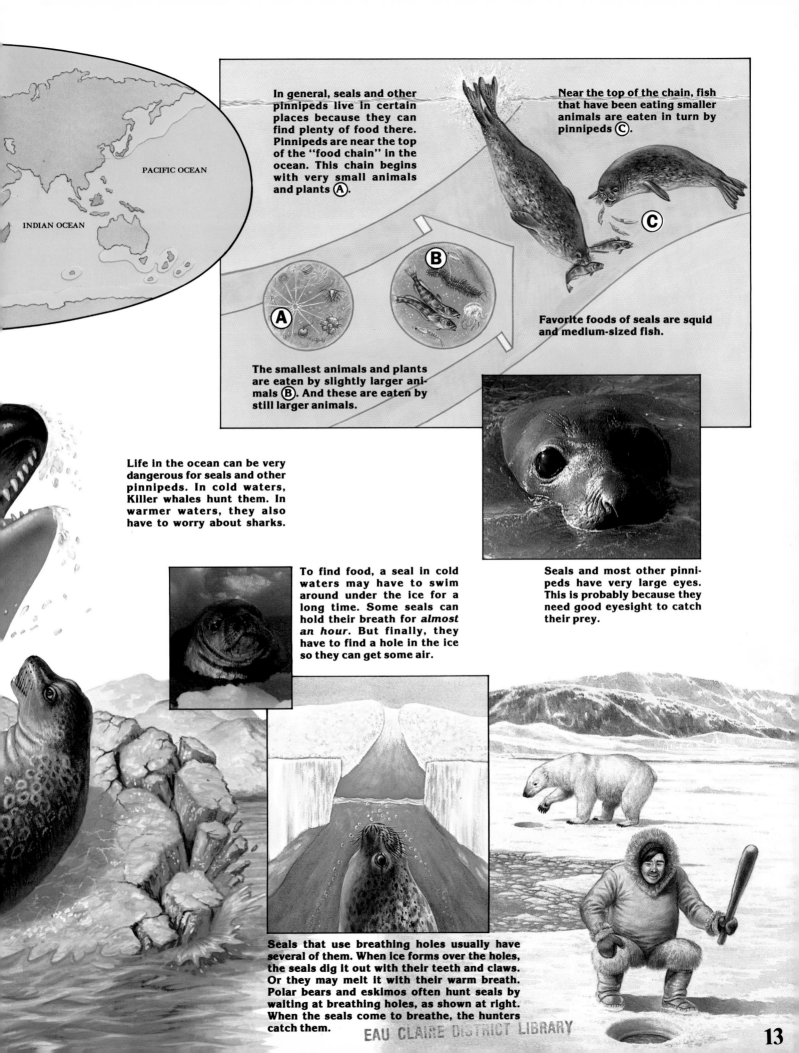

Sea lions and fur seals are very closely related to each other. In fact, they look so much alike and behave in such a similar way that scientists think of them as a single family.

But there are some differences between them. For one thing, sea lions usually have shorter snouts than fur seals. And the fur on sea lions is usually shorter and thinner. The fur on fur seals can be so long and thick that they are often called "sea bears."

All adult male sea lions and fur seals are much larger than the females. And male sea lions often have manes of hair on their heads, as shown below.

PACIFIC OCEAN

When they come out of the water, fur seals and sea lions usually choose rocky beaches as places to rest. Unlike seals and walruses, fur seals like this one don't like to lie down on snow and ice.

Sea lions got their name from the hairy manes that adult males have. These sometimes look very much like the manes of African lions.

When a big male sea lion stalks down the beach on its flippers (below), it can look remarkably like an African lion.

Baby sea lions have to stay out of the way of the huge adult males. The males can have very bad tempers, and they sometimes step on the young or injure them in other ways.

Places where sea lions and fur seals live are shown in yellow.

ATLANTIC OCEAN

PACIFIC OCEAN

INDIAN OCEAN

Like true seals, sea lions and fur seals may live in rather cold places. But most of them stay away from the very coldest areas, near the North and South poles.

Sea lions and other pinnipeds may spend days in the water, without going on land. For this reason, they have ways of sleeping in the water. In shallow water, they may sink to the bottom and sleep while holding their breath. They rise to the surface from time to time to get some air, then sink again. In deeper water, they may float upright with just the tip of their noses above water, as shown below.

California sea lions and some other pinnipeds are famous for their ability to balance things on their noses. They can learn these tricks fairly easily, and this indicates that they are intelligent animals. Some scientists think that pinnipeds may be as intelligent as cats or monkeys.

When the skins of fur seals are made into coats, they look very pretty on people. But the skins look even better on the seals, where they belong.

Fur seals have been killed by the millions to get their thick and soft fur. This fur is so much thicker than the fur of other pinnipeds because it has many more hairs, as shown at left. In addition to the long hairs that all pinnipeds have Ⓐ, fur seals also have many shorter hairs Ⓑ. The shorter hairs are called *underfur*.

These Cape Fur Seals have gathered in large protective numbers to give birth to and care for their young.

19

Walruses are really quite different from other pinnipeds in many ways. Unlike the others, walruses have long white tusks. They have short stiff whiskers, and small pig-like eyes. And they have very little hair on their huge bodies.

It's hard to say if walruses are more closely related to seals or to sea lions. Like seals, they use their rear flippers to push them when they swim. But they also use their front flippers, like sea lions.

Male walruses can be very large. They are sometimes more than 12 feet long (3.7 meters). And they may weigh more than 3500 pounds (1600 kilograms). That's as much as *23 fully grown men*. Female walruses are smaller, but still rather large. They usually weigh about 1500 pounds.

Almost all pinnipeds like to crow together in large groups. When group is in the water, it is called *herd*. When it is on land, it is calle a *rookery*.

All pinnipeds have little tails between their rear flippers. But the walrus is the only one that has a flap of skin that connects the tail to the flippers.

The wonderful tusks of a walrus are really just two teeth in the upper jaw that grow very large. As long as a walrus keeps living, its tusks keep growing. And they can sometimes become very long. On a large walrus, the tusks can be *3 feet long* (1 meter) and weigh over 13 pounds (6.3 kilograms).

Walruses use their tusks to find food on the bottom of the ocean. They stir up the mud on the bottom to see if shellfish are hiding in it (as shown at right). The tusks are also used as weapons when two walruses fight, or when they fight other animals.

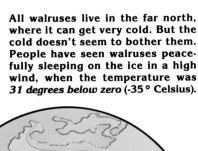

All walruses live in the far north, where it can get very cold. But the cold doesn't seem to bother them. People have seen walruses peacefully sleeping on the ice in a high wind, when the temperature was *31 degrees below zero* (-35° Celsius).

NORTH POLE

RUSSIA

ALASKA

Places where walruses live are shown in yellow.

To help them float in the water, walruses have air pouches around their necks. These can be filled with air, like human life preservers.

Walruses use their "life preservers" to keep them floating when they don't feel well, or when they want to sleep at sea. The huge amount of blubber in their bodies also helps to keep them floating, since fat floats in sea water.

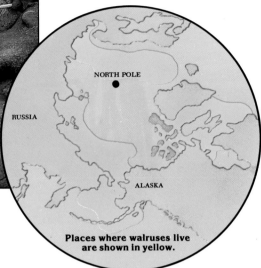

Walrus whiskers are often used to find food. In the dark at the bottom of the ocean, walruses use their whiskers like fingers to feel around in the mud for food. A walrus has about 300 thick, stubby whiskers.

The skin on the neck and shoulders of a walrus is extra thick. On a male, it can be almost 3 inches thick (7 centimeters). Males have huge bumps on this part of their bodies, but females do not.

The tusks of walruses are very valuable. Like the tusks of elephants, they can be used for carving. For this reason, walrus tusks are often called walrus "ivory." For hundreds of years, people killed walruses for their ivory, and made it into many things. This 12th Century chess piece is one beautiful example.

Today, it is against the law in most places to hunt walruses. But eskimos are still allowed to hunt them, because walrus meat and blubber are a traditional part of the eskimo food supply. To make sure that the eskimos don't take too many walruses, they can only hunt with spears and other old fashioned hunting equipment. They cannot use guns.

How does a walrus scratch its head? With its tail, of course. Walruses may look too big and fat to do this. But they have very flexible backbones, like all pinnipeds.

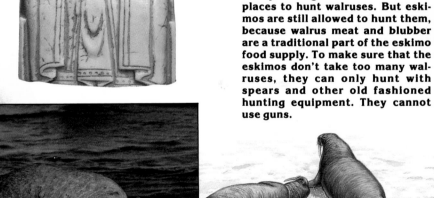

The future of pinnipeds looks much brighter today that it once did. At one time, about a hundred years ago, it seemed certain that almost all of the seals, sea lions and walruses in the world were going to be destroyed by human hunters. But today, it appears that most species of pinnipeds are out of danger.

Like whales, pinnipeds were hunted during the 19th Century for the oil that could be made out of their body fat. This oil was used in lamps, before electric lights were invented. Millions of seals and other pinnipeds were boiled down to provide oil for the lamps of the world.

Unlike whales, many pinnipeds were also hunted for their fur. And walruses were killed for their beautiful ivory tusks. These things were so valuable that millions of pinnipeds were killed *every year* to get them.

The greed of the hunters was so great that they often didn't bother to leave enough animals alive to breed new animals. As a result, the numbers of many pinniped species fell rapidly. Fur seals of all kinds were nearly wiped out. Elephant seals came very close to extinction. Some seal species did become extinct.

Then, several things happened that helped to save the pinnipeds. First, the hunters killed so many members of some species that there were no longer enough animals left to justify the expense of hunting them. So these species were left alone. At the same time, electric lights were invented and the market for seal oil began to dry up. And finally, governments around the world started to make laws to protect pinnipeds.

As a result of all these things, the numbers of most pinniped species have grown larger in recent years. With some species, such as Northern fur seals, there may be as many animals alive today as there were before all the hunting began.

This is very good, but all pinniped species are still not completely safe. For example, the Soviet Union still allows the killing of seals and walruses in certain areas. And Canada allows the hunting of Harp seals.

Certainly, it is time for *all* hunting of pinnipeds to stop. Unlike the people of the 19th Century, we don't need oil from pinnipeds. And we have many ways to cloth ourselves without taking skins from wild animals. Living pinnipeds are far more valuable today than dead ones.

Index